Poems 2023.

1. Van Gogh Sky.
2. Withering Wind.
3. Robert Shaw.
4. Holy Alien.
5. Confused.
6. Don't care.
7. You forgot your snap tin Jimmy.
8. AI.
9. Penny worth o Kali.
10. Park at Twilight.
11. Decimal.
12. Doves, wasps and hedgehogs.
13. Memories of the Building Game.
14. Books.
15. Stream become a river.
16. Mister Universe.
17. Maths for Fred.
18. Gloating.

19. Jasper and Jenny.

20. Difficult Rhymes.

21. Collective Nouns.

22. Dear Grandad.

23. Progressive.

24. T'Northern Route.

25. The Shed in France.

26. New Democracy.

27. Neuralyzer.

28. Thingy's Sister.

29. Rules.

30. Why do you exist.

31. Poetry.

32. Cults.

33. God regretted creating us.

34. Chateau Boneworks.

35. What Shall I Wear?

36. Far Right.

37. Siamese Heritage.

38. Bolton Fish Market.

39. We Played Here.

40. Unneeded.

41. Conspiracy Theorist.

42. The Amish.

43. Tightrope of Sanity.

44. Painted Sunset.

45. Quentin.

46. On the Right Track.

47. The Magician.

48. My life in a flower.

49. Son of a Bitch (1)

50. Stop in or go't Disco?

51. Rock on the Moon.

52. mafia.

53. Sick Budgie.

54. Thought Control.

55. Different Answer.

56. Tree Grieves.

57. Two Crying Onions.

58. Lil's Cafe.

59. Girls I took to the pictures in the 70's.

60. St. Thomas's Social Club.

61. Haiku.

62. Altar Boy.

63. Flies.

64. Art Awreet?

65. Bergerac.

66. Old Boat.

67. Down a Cobbled Street.

68. What is it?

69. Burn the Witch.

70. The Rucks.

71. 12 'o clock Hill.

72. Zombie Apocalypse.

73. Emperor's New Clothes.

74. Impossible.

75. Son of a Bitch (2).

76. The Goodies.

77. The Boneworks.

78. Gone.

79. 15 Minute City.
80. Perfect.
81. Corridor.
82. Misdirection.
83. Women's Day.
84. Question Everything.
85. Ministry of truth.
86. Bommy.
87. Black Clad Goons.
88. Rat in my Mind.
89. Jackson Pollock.
90. Computer Says No.
91. Pouring Rain.
92. H
93. End o't World.
94. Another Dream Day.
95. Carol Vorderman's ****
96. Wheer?
97. Honest Truth.
98. New Year, New Brain.

99. Don't Comply.
100. Sorry.
101. Irish.
102. Evaporating Kiss.
103. Snow.
104. Murdered Bird.
105. Pontificating.
106. Today's
107. Trying to Help.
108. Alexa.
109. Made in China.
110. Something Better.
111. Messy Peas.
112. My New French Song.
113. On the Couch.
114. Where is the Drink in This.
115. Last Day of Summer.
116. Raindrops don't Lie.
117. Forged the Copper Brussel's Sprouts.
118. Woman Crossin't Road.

119. Nature's Soup.

120. Little Blue Shoes.

121. Little Shoes (2)

122. It Was Something.

123. Pushing Forty.

124. Get a Kitten.

125. Back Street Pubs.

126. Half Past Six.

127. barn Owl.

128. Bat Shit Truth.

129. Witchwalking.

130. Ode to a Fly.

131. Town Hall Steps.

132. Brave Pal.

133. This Place is Crawling with Phantoms.

134. Beltane.

135. Down and Out.

136. Get It?

Collection 2023

1.

Woke at three to a Van Gogh sky

Pictured in the bedroom window frame

Moon illumed the curling cavalier clouds

Flares of light the distant stars aflame

The yellows and the blues

The waterfalls of light

The silhouettes and shadows inky black

The custard crescent moon

The tidal waves of night

Why can't my real days be just like that.

2.

I went for a walk in the withering wind

The wood wrecking wind was writhing

The tree branches, twigs, leaves and scurrying things

The withering wind was scything

Fresh thoughts blew through my half asleep mind

Connecting electric brain wires

Memories flew on the scent of the sea

Sung by angels in sky wind choirs

I went for a walk in the withering wind

With lost times I tried to revive

But I don't need the old days in this brand new fresh storm

It is so good to just be alive.

3.

Robert Shaw

A Man for all Seasons he came from King street

Born 9th of August 1927

A childhood in Howfen, fifty one years later

In Toormakeady he left us for heaven

Such a short life for an artistic giant

Actor, novelist, screen writer, playwright

Larger than life, yet creative and gentle

A thinker, a father, as deep as the night.

From Russia with love Red the Bond villain

Claudius in Hamlet, Custer of the West

Force 10 from Navarone, Martin Luther

Macbeth, Cymbeline and all the rest

In Battle of the Bulge he was German Hessler

As Doyle Hannigan he was stung in The Sting

A man for all Season as Henry VIII

From King street the man who would be king.

"You know, the thing about a shark, he's got lifeless eyes,

black eyes, like a doll's eyes.

He'll take ya whole, swallow ya whole."

When he said it we were all petrified.

Quint sang: "Here lies the body of Mary Lee;

 died at the age of a hundred and three.

For fifteen years, she kept her virginity;

not a bad record for this here vicinity."

Then bleak horror USS Indianapolis

The description of that only he could emote

To sail alongside him to float in his waters

We're all going to need a bigger boat.

Farewell and adieu to you Fair Spanish ladies

Farewell and Adieu Robert Archibald Shaw

Proud son of Howfen remembered forever

For more than just the voice from the Jaw.

4.

The holy alien.

When the aliens land will they have spindly arms

Or muscles like Arnold Schwarzenegger

Will they be clad in svelte chromium suits

Or like a barbarian celestial beggar

Will their brains be multiple of Einstein power

Or ordinary controlled by machines

Will they be so scientifically superior

That their faces won't be glued to little screens

Will they be really soft and benevolent

Or shred us with the viciousness of space

Will they think us less than we think of germs

Or will they treat us with charity and grace

Will their leader be a tyrant of unbridled power

Or will he die for us like Jesus in the scroll

Allowing us to live, allowing us to sin

Then dissolving into a vision of our soul

5.

Confused.

Just seen Zelensky in Lidl, in Skem

He were with Jordan you know her wit big bust

Everybody looks like somebody else

My powers of ID I can't trust.

I saw Beethoven once in Bolton

Just stood theer wi a dancin instructor

Gerrin ont bus at Moor Lane station

He were havin' a word wit conductor.

Charles Manson, just seed him in Chorley

In Galloways buying two pies

I could see his reflection in cake display glass

Still got them disturbing mad eyes.

What's that wench cawd outa Corrie?

She's been in a few TV progs

She were going through stuff in her handbag

Stood outside of a closed women's bogs.

Just seen yon mon outa U2

Is it bonehole, boneworks or just Bono?

I'm sure he were chattin to John Lennon

Outside Home Bargains waiting for Yoko Ono.

6.
Don't care what other people think of you.

Don't give their ego shoulders a rub.

Just use your inner common sense of caring,

You don't need to belong to any club.

There is no honest left or right reality.

All global leaders, not one worth a bean.

Love your family, respect your fellow man,

Keep your side of the good street clean.

Don't jump on their political bandwagons.

Don't worry about the things they tell you to.

To them your just a meaningless statistic,

To be mixed up in their selfish control stew.

Don't wear their badges or fly their media flags

Don't obey them, with your brain they're messing

Don't answer any of their faux moral questions.

Don't respond just keep the bastards guessing.

Turn off the television, don't buy papers.

They want your kids and grandkids, not just you.

Be kind to all God's creatures and be grateful

For each blessed day under the brittle blue.

7.

You forgot your snap tin Jimmy

But you won't need it now

Not since the gas thundered up the mine and spit you out

Not since the rock belched fury and melted your little soul

You won't need it any more

The mornings will not call you

Nor your mates wait for you

Your bed will be hollow

My heart is empty and wrecked

My son, thirteen

Working in a hard man's world

But the money will still filter up

To the pockets of those who need it least

While the children in the belly of the beast

Get roasted, broken and lost

An inconvenient cost

But words will be said at a very high level

Yes very strong words will be said

In the corridors of power

And heads will be nodded and letters signed

But you forgot your snap tin Jimmy

Never mind.

8.

AI

There is nothing quite so false

As something which looks nearly true

That picture is very similar

But it is not quite, not quite you.

In fact that missing little something

Makes the whole seem a profanity

Tainting every sinister advance

Lacking truth, lacking love, lacking humanity.

9.

I don't want a red Ferrari that goes 200 round a bend

I don't want a tattoo to make me look more mannish

I just want to have what I had when I were ten

A penny worth a kali and an ha'penny spanish.

I don't want a beachfront villa in the Caribbean

I don't want a magic ring to make me vanish

I just want to be stood theer outside o't wooden hut

Wi a penny worth a kali and an ha'penny spanish

You can shove your Armani suits and your fake tans

I don't need my food to taste a bit more Japanish

I just want to dip my little stick in American cream soda

Wi mi penny worth o kali and an ha'penny spanish

I don't want to be in your gang or anybody else's

I like it on me own I'm not that clannish

Standin' theer full o dreams in 1962

Wi mi penny worth o kali and an ha'penny spanish.

You can take away mi English nationality

I don't fit in, throw me away, I'll take the banish

As long as ahve geet me lips coated in sugar

Wi mi penny worth a kali and an ha'penny spanish.

10.

The dead flower blows into the gutter

Paper leaves swirl across the grass

The evening drifting lonely in the park

All the golden days of loving surely pass

The bus stop glares with cheap graffiti

Broken glass, crushed cans beneath the seat

Twilight hanging in't cafe window

Empty table where they used to meet

Little dog looks up into her face

Where we going mummy, its got late

Nothing for us here my true companion

Symbolic noise, the closing of the gate

God its hard, its cold, the noisy city

So many people living in their phone

Sunlight paints a path across the pavement

Thin wind blows the sound of being alone.

11.

Can ya lend us two and two till Thursday

Ahve only geet half a crown

Gi us that ahl gi thee fourpence back

Feel int pocket then a frown

Ahve only geet three haypence on mi

Ahl owe thee tuppence haypenny awreet?

Aye ant two and two as weal don't forget

Ahl gi it thi don't worry Thursday neet

Cont change this haypney fer two farthings

Awreet but this ones dilapidated

They say were gooin decimal next year

Ahm dreading that, it'll make things complicated.

12.

All the doves are revolting

They're planning a coo

Pigeons are not happy

They're considering one too

I find wasps a bit stripey

But generally gentle

Today's first of September

When all wasps go mental

All through the summer

They had a purpose in life

Now sugarless and pointless

They sharpen bum knife

From April to August

Their food was abundant

Now they're all starving

And they've been made redundant

Swallows are resting

On the telegraph wires

Watch out for hedgehogs

When your lighting bonfires.

13.

Memory of the building game.

For twelve young years I worked with brickies

Labourers with leather hands and faded blue tattoos

Enamel cups of steaming tea on a plank

Sat round a fire of burning pallets in Winter

There the sweat of ale and workhard muscle

Mingled with the yarns and jokes at brew time

For all their faults and all their unrefined talk

Their busted boots and cement grey jeans

The cussing and false fights and mockery

I felt more honesty there than any

In the lie infested corridors of board rooms and offices

Brew time brief and back up ladders

Fresh wind echoed the sound of demolishing walls

Mixers starting up and a hod being filled.

14. Books

Life was thumping my belly, my world had just died.

I got that good book and I crawled inside.

Slap chains of hail storms swiped and laughed in my face

Inside that book I could hide my disgrace

The hatred, the despair, the torment, the rages

A new novel lifted me up with its pages

When reality hurts like a hot acid knife

Get a good book, for a moment ditch life.

When she starts acting like a velociraptor

It's time to turn over to the next chapter

When people hate you and scorn you

Give you grief and dirty looks … Get books.

15.

When does a stream become a river

When does a pond become a lake

When does a sea become an ocean

When does a snack become T bone steak

When does a shitzu become a wolfhound

When does a drunken thought become a viral Tweet

When does a tiddler become a great white shark

When does a chair become a three piece suite

When does a kitten become a rabid sabre toothed tiger

When does I feel really great become depression

When does I've put on a few ounces become five stone

When does I'll just have one become an all night session

When does a hill become a mountain

When does truth become the last resort

When does I love you and want to spend the rest of my life with you

Turn into I hate you and I'll see you in court.

16.

Mister Universe.

Nothing we observe is really real

It is just our interpretation of reality

We call that dog, we call that moon

But our names and labels are no guarantee

That if a creature from another world

Saw the very same things as us

They would call a spade a spade

Or a tin box full of people a bus.

But that's just names for things that we observe

I'm trying to get much deeper in this verse

We're made of atoms from the depths of space

So that muscle man is really Mr Universe.

17.

Maths for Fred.

Is Mathematics a gift from God in Heaven

Where 6.999 is nearly but not quite number seven

Where complex quadratic equations bring me to my knees

Yet I can admire the simple beauty of the isosceles

Living on this planet sometimes makes me paranoid

But Maths says worry not, its just an oblate spheroid

Orbiting round the sun using differentiation

But how did we invent that explanation?

Something clicked behind Isaac Newton's specs

Simple, profound worth a googolplex

Of money, of elegance, tames my beating heart

But you can't explain that gift with a pie chart.

18.

It is very hot here today and I'm not gloating.

I'll be doing lots of swimming, well actually floating.

In my speedos and my shades with skin turned gold

I have the body of a Greek god, well it looks 3000 years old.

Now I'm approaching forty I must look my best

Lots of exercise this morning, well I did get dressed.

Then into my fitness regime, I am no slouch

Three hours on the treadmill, well I mean the couch.

Eat only pro-biotic healthfood before the footy

Three cans of lager, salted nuts and a bacon butty.

It takes a lot of dedication to look this fine

So I'll keep off the vodka until half time.

19.

Jasper and Jenny.

Ring for the butler Jenny dear

This cushion needs adjusting

Certainly Jasper, just a tick

Need the loo, I'm ruddy busting

Orf she went and back she came

The butler for to bell

In came Clarence, alas too late

"Its adjusted its bloody self!"

While you're here dear boy piped up Jasp

Fix me a gin and tonic

Certainly sir! "And shut that door"

That draught is damned cyclonic.

Life is bloody hard said Jasper

I'm about to vent my spleen!

I don't know how we bloody manage here

Not a patch on Hindley Green.

20.

Difficult Rhymes.

Don't talk to me in duck billed platitudes

Yeah, I'm speaking to thee Belinda

Lookin at me like something the cat he chewed

Stop tryin't catch wasps in a colander.

Sufferin' Sasquatch you've got big feet, she cried

Tha could give th'Hobbits a game wi them buggers

Your feet look cute in them trainers, he lied

Trot off, make me a coffee, two sugars

Mek it thiself you cheeky young snipe

Sittin theer like a fat praying mantis

Me fat! Look at thee, if tha fell int sea

You couldn't be rescued by't Mon from Atlantis

I'm not being insulted by t'likes o thee

Why? Are there better insulters available?

Must admit you're a leading Insultee

In fact I think your lead is unassailable

Get out of this house and never return!

She opened t'door, her face could stand riveting

Howd on a bit love you know this is my house

Remember you were just visiting

Time fer a couple more insults each

You know really I think you're one in a million

So are you sweety she passed by out of reach

But so is a one eyed crocodilian.

21.

A murder of crows are waiting on your shed

A piteousness of doves white out your wall

Being watched closely by a glaring of cats

Will a nest of rumours be your last downfall

Across the road a waddling of ducks sets off

Disturbing ugh! a business of flies

The last leftovers of a cauldron of hawks

Poor mischief of rats where the last one dies

A consortium of octopi avoid a shiver of sharks

A rhumba of rattlesnakes snare drum the beat

Nothing better than a convergence of kinkajous

To muse collective nouns in the summer heat.

22.

Dear Grandad,

8/8/2035

I hope this letter finds you safe and well in heaven. You would not like what is going on here. Do you remember when there used to be two main parties Labourer and the Con thingy. Well they are all the same now. They still pretend to be different but it feels like they are working for somebody else and not the people who vote? Well that's what my mum says. You can't say anything against the leaders now or they close your bank account and make all your cash disappear. Some big men all dressed in black came round last night and took Daddy away for a holiday, that's what they said anyway and I don't think he wanted to go, he didn't even have a suitcase. All the teachers have gone funny too. Some of the alright nice ones got sent to the same holiday camp as Daddy and the ones that are left just keep saying the same things all the time and if we say anything they say we will go to the children's club in Bolton. Tommy got sent there and nobody has seen him since not even his mum. Two of the teachers are them new robots now. They do arithmetic and sex. I don't like them. Do you know when you used to have a car, well only special people can have them now and everybody else just walks. But it is ok because everything we need is close by. You wouldn't like the food either, it is gnats and mealworms I think squashed into paste and made into nice shapes like hearts and stars but there is no farms now. The leaders needed the land for the factories and the holiday camps. Billy Robert's dad went mad and tried to set fire to the Party headquarters. He is gone now. I say my prayers every night like you told me to. Can you come back from heaven and sort all this out cos mum is very sad. Love Mary x

23.

Progressive.

I've got African friends and they'd give me a smack

If I said your villages and towns are too black

But I've checked with the Beeb and they say that its right

English towns and villages are just too white

And the little children who are born with white skin

They are also born with original sin

Its not enough to say that we're all the same

No the little white ones should carry some shame

And if that's not enough in their complex young life

If they want to change gender we can help with a knife

And your Mummies and Daddies are such a disgrace

Saying drag queens shouldn't twerk in your face

What do they know, they're all far too possessive

Get with the new world and the word is progressive

You can call me a bigot you can call me right wing

But the innocent ones don't need political spin

They need love and stability at home and at school

Not used as a progressive globalist tool.

24.

T'northern route.

Think ahl do t'northern route toneet

Call int Grapes then Starkie early back door

Then up to Commercial, after walk up street

That pub opposite Piggy Taylors is no more

Pint o Walkers bitter int th'Horseshoe

Have some laughs wit t'other early drinkers

Slide across to Greyhound such a trek!

Then't Dog and Pheasant mixing with the thinkers

Cross the owd A6 and visit Windmill

Have a chat with Stuart behind the bar

Then on t'ot Waggon an Horses if I must

Funny ale but I'll have another jar

Look at clock tickin but there's still time

To call in um all again on mi way back

Quiet drinkin on a Tuesday neet

Get to weekend we'll have some proper craic.

25.

The Shed in France.

Cleaning the old wood shed out in France

Not been done since the end of the Middle Ages

Hornets, wasps, mosquitoes led me a merry dance

Giant centipedes, spiders, big enough for cages

Empty bottle of Ricard covered in dust

Mowers, strimmers, spades, bits of fence

Saws, axes, hammers, mattocks, ancient boots

Discarded projects in bits that made no sense

The more you move the more the things you find

Hammer horror cobwebs halt my advance

Wine racks with bottles of Chateau Plonk

Guarded by a huge fat toad, only in France

Emaciated tractor held up by rust

Nameless tools abandoned by a nameless farmer

Only things I sadly failed to discover

A sword, a chest of gold and a suit of armour.

26.

New Democracy.

Just get a group of super rich influentials

Who have shared plans for the future of the earth

Through their mega money lending corporations

Like the Mafia they control your life from birth

They infiltrate the governments, civil service

They control the banks, the media and the press

They buy the science and silence non believers

They play with mankind like a game of chess

Through top down management their evil spreads

Like cancer in the unlikeliest of places

Universities, schools and even churches

Medicine, institutions, moral mazes

They create a set of rules you must obey

So good and caring makes a grown man weep

Pitting one against the other weakens both

Till all thats left are brainwashed docile sheep

Split up families, separate out the kids

Belittle everything that once was great

Confusion, fear, reporting your neighbour

Make everyone dependant on the state

Stifle culture, silence creatives, renegades

Use technology make you think you are still free

Demonise real goodness and common sense

And then they call it yes! Democracy.

27.

The Neuralyzer.

Tha knows that sci fi film Men in Black

When whoosh! Wi a little light held in his fist

Then t'other mon cawnt recall a single thing

Its called a Neuralyzer and they exist!

I just found me self stood in kitchen, no idea

How I got theer with a glass of lukewarm Tizer

I must have been abducted by some aliens

Then they zapped me with a bloody Neuralyzer

Then t'other neet I were stood at top o't stairs

I looked from left to right, which way to go?

Th'aliens had neuralyzed me again

How I'd got theer I don't bloody know.

Sat'day neet I walked in very late

Wife were standin' theer with a rolling pin

"What bloody time do you call this?"

I said I've been neuralysed then I got bloody neuralysed again!

28.

Thingy's sister.

Yon lady across from't chippy's her's awreet

If she were crossin't road I would assist her

An that wench who used tek papers up my street

I like her but nor as much as Thingy's sister.

That woman who does t'weather abeawt tea time

If I had a weather channel I'd enlist her

Then talk abeawt high pressure un isobars

But I'd rather do that wi Thingy's sister.

I like that Welsh wench too wit long red hair

That town her comes from its a right tongue twister

But even with her international charms

Her's not a patch at all on Thingy's sister.

Ah seed her all dressed up, she'd washed her hair

She were limping, new wellies, gorra blister

I've never met her let alone bloody kissed her

Burra don't half fancy tha knows Thingy's sister.

29.

Rules.

I used to love wagging school

Walking around Bolton in the rain

All the teachers thought I was a fool

If I was back there I'd do it all again.

Some rules make obvious perfect sense

Like don't drive cars when you're steaming drunk

But sometimes they who must be obeyed

Must be ignored and their rules debunked

Look at the people making all the laws

Are they thinking of the best for you and yours

Or have they got another plan attached

When they tell you what to eat and stay indoors

Common sense and just morality

Will help you through the decision making fog

Meanwhile as a rule of thumb

Just try and emulate this dog.

30.

Why do you exist?

You lie through enamelled teeth

You infect all the air we breath

You smile the false neon smile

Trying to hide your rising bile

You rule with the velvet fist

Why do you exist?

Your intelligence is forged in hell fire

You wear the suit of a professional liar

In rooms where you plan your things

There are people hanging up from rings

Please keep me off your list.

Why do you exist?

Not one hair is out of place.

You look like a model for the word disgrace.

Armani trousers, cross your legs

While the working man outside works and begs.

I see you through a bloody mist.

Why do you exist?

False morals cloak your every word

Your plans should seem so absurd

But the people just play along

They think that they must be wrong

But that's the point they missed.

Why do you exist?

Let's pray for renegades today

Who won't listen, who won't obey

Who'll protest with marching feet

Who'll fill the parks and fill the streets

While you hide in a cupboard and slit your wrists

Why do you exist?

Your plans, your future plans

Don't include the nobility of the working man

Your world is without soul

All that matters is your control.

If you died, I think I'd just get pissed

Why do you exist?

31.

Poetry.

Poetry loves words like marmalade and slutch

Mop out your morning mind like a soothsayer

Then buzz, skrike, bong, shriek, zapp and tinkle, tonk

Your ears prick up to onomatopoeia

Slide the soft sweet senses, sing the sumptuous sounds

Can't beat a bit of bare alliteration

Sonnets, haiku, limericks, elegies, odes

Elation, admiration of the nation

Shakespeare, Milton, Donne, Michelle, Mick and Dryden

Poets pouring plethoras of poignancy

Then trying to find a rhyme, don't take too much time,

There's nothing actually rhymes with poignancy

So what is the point of this morning's mithering

Why bother ever putting pen to paper?

Don't watch the news, just find a muse, like singing the blues

Better than jumping off the next skyscraper.

32.

Cults.

Charlie Manson's gang

Jimmy Jones and Heaven's Gate

Ones who lie and kill to get results

Cults.

Dark robed groups in cellars

Burning candles waxing black

Brainwashed mystic followers of occults

Cults

The Branch Davidians

Manipulated people in their sway

Praying to false prophets group exults

Cults

Teaching little children

The sexual theories of the day

Treating little innocents like adults

Cults

33.

God regretted creating us

What I'm saying is not libel

My friend Ekpe reminded me

It's there in Genesis in the Bible

He made us then he watched us

And he saw what we could do

He decided to terminate us

Time to close this human zoo

Time to drown all his mistakes

And their wicked society

Then he saw a single person

Who lived with blameless piety

So he gave us one more chance

He risked Noah and the Ark

To be the future of humanity

Take us to light from dark

Did he make the right decision?

Have we gone from bad to good

Take a look around you brothers

Maybe time for the next flood.

34.

Chateau Boneworks.

Where were you the night the Boneworks closed

Oh Lord I'll miss them pongs

They reached to Blackrod and Chequerbent

And as far south as Tyldesley Bongs

Sometimes it were so strong you could taste it

Unique like a vintage wine

You could bottle it and give it people you hate

"Here, you'll love this '59"

The '63 were a classic year too

You could smell it stuck to your clothes

Rotting flesh and intestines

Full bodied with a complex nose.

35.

What shall I wear?

Funerals and weddings

And other grand affairs

I'm always at a loss

To know which clothes to wear

But seeing all the people

Not seen since the last one

Can be a quick reminder

Who's still here and who has gone

Then between the church and hall

Nip outside for a fag and breather

And realise deep down

I'm not too keen on either

Not because of lack of love

Or respect you want to pay

Its just the fact that love and life

Don't revolve around one day

If I had to choose between them

Death of owd Tommy or marriage of daughter

I think I'll pick the former

Cos funerals are shorter!

36.

Far right.

These days truth is lies

And day is night

In this newspeak I'm far right

I always wore a left wing hat

Look after the underdogs, stuff like that

Stand up for the working class

Fight against the ones with brass

Be proud of the men who built this land

Who dug int pit with their spades and hands

The women breathing dust so rotten

Int factories and mills wit cotton

The unions who stood for worker's rights

The strikers and the picket fights

Someone stole the old left wing

And made of it a grotesque thing

Owned by the elite and the media liars

In Knightsbridge and the gleaming spires

Used to lever political will

To shame the ones who believe still

The family and the rights of the free

That's what left wing means to me

When you treat everyone the same

Phobias and isms can't be blamed

I went to sleep one distant night

Dreaming left I woke up far right.

37.

"Disagreement regarding Siamese heritage"

She said "Is there anybody here from Siam?"

I said "I am"

She said "You don't look like you're from Siam"

I said "I am"

We went for our dinner

She had lamb and I had Spam

We both had toast with jam

She was thinking, he's not from Siam

I was thinking, I am.

Hometime

I was walking behind a woman with a pram

She went past stood up on a tram

She mouthed "You're not from Siam"

I mouthed "I am".

(I am going through my Abstract Pointless Poems phase. It has to be done)

38.

Bolton Fish Market.

They say tales grow in the telling

And I'm sure that some of them will

But I'll tell you a tale that my mother told me

Because it lives in my memories still.

Bridge street, Bolton 1932

The fish market had been there many years

Council decided it must be demolished

They started, then they saw them big ears.

Out of the dust the biggest rat came

Followed by hundreds of others

Big uns and little uns black uns and grey

Rat families, sisters and brothers.

They stretched across all of Bridge street

In formation, a gigantic V

With the king rat at front o't procession

A marvel for all folks to see.

People ran and hid in shop doorways

As rats passed they pulled in their feet

With the giant rat at front they marched on

Till they came to Ashburner street.

That's were they'd built the new fish market

Who told the rats? well nobody knows

Police had to deal with the shock and the fear

And that's how the story goes.

My mother told me that tale one night

And I listened with eyes staring blue

But I've just looked it up on old Google

And bloody hell yes, it is true!

39.

We played here last night.

It wasn't full like the glory days

But what a great thing to do

To be stood where greats have stood

Making people laugh and sing

From that stage every smiling face was visible

When they turned the spotlights off

And the vastness of the place and its history

Made me think how lucky I was

Just to be there one more time.

40.

Unneeded.

Paths overgrown with nettles and brambles

Stiles and gates rotting, broken, unneeded

How long since someone passed by this way

Breathing the silence with mansworld unheeded

There! a swift weasel and nobody saw it

Artistic landscape and no-one to draw it

Transcendent sunset the colours of dreams

While everyone seems to be glued to their screens

Thank God I don't have a mobile phone

Thank God I don't have a telly

Thank God I've got a warm, dry place to sleep

And just enough, just enough food in my belly.

41.

You knew it was coming and you said nothing

They called me Conspiracy Theorist

But you knew it was coming and you said nothing

People were not interested, they had their lives

But you said nothing and you knew

I couldn't corroborate, conflicting stories

It was there to see but everyone was distracted

But now it is too late and you said nothing

I tried but hardly anyone was interested

The brainwashing was too powerful

The people, in vast numbers, so gullible

But you said nothing

Oh I did, but nobody heard me.

I didn't want to cause any arguments or lose friends

If you had tried harder maybe more would have realised

But you knew it was coming and you said nothing.

I thought someone else would do it.

42.

The Amish.

No I don't want your app to park my bloody car

I don't want a silicone chip in my arm

I don't want to be part of your technological world

I'm going back to the farm

I'm sick of all your computerised advances

Make me jump through hoops they're all so so samish

I'm donning a hat and I'm growing a beard

I'm joining The Amish.

Stick your TV licence where the sun don't shine

I don't want your Tesco club points either

Some people are slaves to their mobile phones

Download this App! Give me a breather

Won't eat your meat made in a laboratory

I want free range eggs and I take my bacon Danish

Stick your Mrna and your sexual deviances

I'm joining the Amish

I want a job where I'm chopping logs

Not working from home doing some bloody accounts

I don't need The Science to tell me its pissing down

Using words that I can't pronounce

Smart motorways my arse why is there always a jam

I know I always sound a bit blamish

But for avoidance of doubt, I'm bailing out

I'm joining The Amish.

That blokes a woman, that politician's a crook

Confused people's lives are train wrecked

I have to watch every word I come out with

Or I'll be arrested for being politically incorrect

They want digital ID to make me prove who I am

I'm Jim, james, Jacques, Jimmy, Hamish

I've had enough of 1984

I'm joining The Amish.

43.

He was manicuring his character

Balanced between self hatred and vanity

Wondering where did the muse go

Creative explosions or inanity

Confused by his mystical childhood

Satanic thoughts no! Christianity

Also confused by most people

Loving none or all of humanity

His good moods and bad moods vocalised

Soft sacred words or profanity

Out in the grey misty morning

Walking the tightrope of sanity.

44.

Smoked the Painted Sunset.

Letter to self: where were you when I needed you most?

Seems like all my hopes and dreams have withered into a ghost.

I was too busy stealing cheap thrills for the trip.

Getting by on delusion, shooting bent from the hip.

Now the bloody dusk light mixed with sky hanging dust.

Bids farewell to a beautiful day - but only just.

Smoked the painted sunset through a little cigar.

Threw the last remains through the window of my car.

Belting down the back roads with my soul on fire.

Analysing memories without being a liar.

False cattle stood like puppets in an open field.

Picture after pictures of my history unpeeled.

Regrets I've had a few, far too many to mention.

All of my self defence soldiers are standing to attention.

Dead Past/Brave Future, here's the fork in the road.

Don't kill baby ducklings whilst avoiding a toad.

Oh a sweet angel barn owl dusted my eyes in the night.

It was then that I knew, despite the past, it's going to be alright.

45.

Quentin.

Quentin was a complex sort of a chappie

He was far too intelligent to ever be happy

He spent his time studying philosophy and such

When asked about pleasure he said no not much

He knew little creatures lived their lives on his face

He knew all the diseases for the whole human race

He studied non-fiction not for him the cheap thrillers

And he knew for the world how many serial killers

Were active or dormant at this moment in time

And the total turned out to be three hundred and nine

He would lie in his bed with his brain calculating

Country by country the mass murder rating

But deep down inside he realised he was ill

But for his kind of malady there was no quick fix pill

When a man has a cold you can tell by his cough

Not easy to see when you can't turn your brain off

He'd got knives, he'd got hammers, screwdrivers of course

And he knew very well just how much blunt force

Would be needed that night to remove a few men

So to turn off his pain he became three hundred and ten.

46.

On the Right Track.

When you don't believe a word from the establishment

When you don't buy papers or watch TV

When you walk alone and you feel isolated

My friend you are starting to be free

When people sneer and laugh at the things you say

When they see you as a joke all the time

But you're looking for the truth and you don't care what they say

My friend you're on the right line.

When you can't be pigeon holed and you can't be understood

When everybody thinks that everything you do's no good

And that bully manager just gave you the sack

My friend you're on the right track.

When the sign says Stop , keep off the grass

When you won't wear all the costumes that you wore in the past

When there's just you and the sky and you get a natural high

Link by link your chains are breaking free.

When you get less friends as each year passes

When people talk about you behind your back

When you spend a little time with those who are lonely

My friend you're on the right track.

When you see more sense in animals than you do in most humans

When you can see you're own weaknesses too

When you try not to judge then you don't have to budge

Stay honest and humble and true.

Thank the Lord in the morning for each wonderful day

When its shining, when its pouring, hot or cold

You've got 24 hours to love the birds and flowers

Getting younger when you think you're getting old.

When you're faced with rules and lectures and authorities advice

And you think no thanks I have finished being nice

And you listen to the people who stand to lose

And you watch what you eat and you watch what you booze

When your heart feels gladness at the laughter of little children

When you help someone and they don't even know

When you don't spend time with false liars in their prime

My friend you are starting to grow.

When you won't join the in crowd or the chattering classes

When you don't go to parties holding champagne glasses

When you're better off in mud up to your knees

My friend you are starting to be free.

When you start to see things clearly for the very first time

You shed the brainwashing lies like a duck sheds slime

The road is straight and true, don't look back

My friend your're on the right track.

47.

The Magician.

He could make things disappear like cigarettes and crates of beer.

Like happiness in his family home, turn colour into monochrome.

His prowess travelled far and wide exceeded only by his pride.

Between the tap room and the gym everything revolved round him.

One trick in the early morn, he woke up, wife and kids had gone.

He could even levitate, he rose above their love with hate.

To gain such skill in the magic arts, he traded in the queen of hearts.

Then one by one through disgust or fear his friends began to disappear.

But one friend never left his side the bottle kept him bleary eyed.

That was perhaps his cleverest trick not realising he was sick.

Then he grew lazy he grew fat, he made it happen just like that.

No friends, no kids, no job, no wife, Abracadabra his magic life.

48.

My life in a flower.

I was in awe when I was young

Standing outside the great pubs that the old men used to drink in

And the train lines and the factories

So many things that I wanted to understand.

How a creature like a man

Could take over the wild lands and cover it in tarmac

Send some men to the moon

While kids in Africa had worms in their eyes.

School and church were just like jail

All my maths was used to calculate the seconds to release

Run across the flags and roads

Into the magic of the streams and fields.

Climbing trees and fishing ponds

Playing cricket in the backs with a dustbin for a wicket

Lifting stones and catching newts

Every day full of wonders all for nowt.

Then when girls came into focus

I was in no doubt at all that I wasn't one of them

Curvy legs shy flirting eyes

They smelled nicer than the lads as well.

Then wagging school and killing time

An expert on Egyptology in Bolton musem.

Wandring streets in the pouring rain

Getting older as the 60's exploded.

I stepped off the spinning waltzer

Realising that I had to leave my childhood days behind me

Down the creaking steps into a new world

Where I was supposed to behave like a man.

Now I'm old I've learned a lot

Not many friends and jobs were pointless had to do it for the money

A loving family is all that matters

So many things I wanted to understand.

49.

Americans always say son of a bitch!

But I've got a different one.

I feel sorry for Tony Blair's mother

Cos she had a bitch of a son.

50.

Stop in or go't Disco?

I've been making some gravy

You know with that instant bisto

Now I can't make me mind up

Should I stop in or go t'Disco

I've still got me hot pants, I can still shake me stuff

Might not be be fair on t'other wenches if I go.

Just tried on me choker

And it choked me a bit more

Bell bottoms and crop tops

Plenty theer in't wardrobe

They're all a bit tighter

Emphasing me curves

I'll put on some lippy, I might go.

I think ahve still got it

Practice spins on the carpet

Balancing on me platforms

Trippin up over the odd pet

I wonder if lads still have taches and affros

Shoulder pads and headbands galore.

Theer ahve found me owd Spandex

Put some glitter round th'eyeballs

Irresistable to't th'opposite sex

Wolfwhistles at nightfall

Ahve still got the time catch that 59 bus

Dancin' in't Beachcomber until dawn.

Think ahl just put kettle on

Have a brew while ahm waiting

Soon ahl be on that sprung floor

With other bodies gyratin

Ahv got beautiful memories and I'm still that same girl

Fallin asleep and dreamin' in me chair.

51.

There is a rock on the moon

That sometimes sits in shade and sits in light

It exists but none of us has seen it

It has no concept of a day or night

It exists in spite of us

It needs not us at all

It exists when humans die

It is unmoved when Empires fall

When wars rage when lovers love

When Shakespeare wrote Othello

And Da Vinci painted Mona Lisa

When lions roar and rhinos bellow

Or sunlight whites the neck of a perfect swan

There is a rock on the moon

And it will still be there when we are gone

52.

The mafia rule by fear and extortion

Blackmail judges, politicians and cops

Psycho elites use the same methods

They find out where the buck stops

They take the World Health Organisation

Then use it to force their control

Faux benevolence covering the steel fist

Virtuous precepts their minions extol

They'll use climate and health and race and gender

Diseases, media narration

To form and shape billions of people

How else to maintain domination

The next one they threaten your children

It's not science, its a political farce

Funny how they win and we lose

Next pandemic? Pandemic my arse.

53.

Sick Budgie.

If ever I get invited out I can never just say no

I always say I'd love to, though I never want to go

Then on the night excuses, the lies I have to tell

Sorry I can't make it, the budgie's not been well.

Using that excuse I know is really rather fudgy

It would have been much better if I'd actually had a budgie

My pet excuse was lame it would have been a better bet

Instead of that lame pet excuse I actually had a lame pet

Because of all the lies I'd told I was starting to lose track

So I bought a real budgie that was a hypochondriac

Now when people phone me up I don't even have to talk

I just put little Joey on and he gives his sickly squawk.

54.

Thought Control

Do you remember when people were good

Well most people I mean

People who you thought you knew a bit

You could agree and disagree

And you didn't have labels and flags

That give you thought castration

Seeing all through mist of attachments

Learned through media subjugation

Seems old fashioned now

To have a difference of opinion

And still be pals and have a laugh

Without their elite dominion

Power doesn't want us to get on

They want us at each other's throats

Disbelievers and heretics

Sharing unscientific anecdotes

He said this, ooh she said that

Like kids in a playground fight

I've had more intelligent conversation

At brew time on a building site

Well I've had enough of politik speak

Mind control, deplatforming, banning

They're coming after you and coming after your kids

It's been a long time in the planning.

55.

He was the only one who got a different answer

All the rest of class had got the same

They were laughing at him voicing the old epithets

Weirdo, billy no mates, lame brain

He wished he'd taken notice of the others

They'd all agreed their answer made more sense

Why did he always misunderstand questions

Must be they're all clever and he's dense

"Stand up lad", the teacher looked so angry

Looked like he was spoiling for a fight

He was ready for the put down and the laughter

Teacher said " How come you're the only one who got this right?"

56.

Tree Grieves.

Is a tree a creature?

Does it have a conscious soul.

From its skyward reaching fingertips

To its heartwood solid bole.

Does it grieve its fallen comrades

When their roots were intertwined

Does it sigh out air at midnight

Is its bulk completely blind.

Having lived ten of our lifetimes

As its life outlives its leaves

When I touch its gnarled bark softly

I feel it, yes it grieves.

57.

Get two crying onions and a broken heart

Put them in a pan of bitter tears

If you have lost the apple of your eye

Forget her with a cupboard full of beers

You have to eat to stay alive

But that's no reason to enjoy it

Fancy pouring gunge inside of you

You have a perfect body don't destroy it.

He sat at the table, sharp knife in his hand

The book of recipes she used to follow

Ripped out every page and threw them in the fire

Didn't want to make a meal of feeling hollow.

58.

She was just a flash of lipstick in a melancholy town

He was Castrol GTX and fading leathers

They were who they had to be in their ordinary lives

But on that bike they were freedom in all weathers

Lil's caff car park Friday evening spinning gravel in the headlights

Coca cola, Elvis on the jukebox

Light blue jeans and blonde quiffs, jet black hair and boots

Speeding on to a lifetime equinox

Now she's a grandmother and he is on his bike

On a Bonneville in heaven riding high

But she's got the pictures and the memories of the speed

Speed of life, my how time does fly.

59.

Girls I took to the pictures in the 70's.

Eva were a disco diva

But her memory for dates were appalling

I'd often be left on me own when

We should have been dance room balling

She promised me she'd try harder

And I tried very hard to believe her

She said remind me again, when are we dancin

I said bloody hell Saturday Night Eva!

Now T she were a smasher

She had an adorable face

I couldn't have found a nicer wench

If I'd looked in outer space

But, as quite often happens

She left me and started to roam.

I often look up at the sky at night

And think Eeh T, come home.

Yin Yang were me Chinese girlfriend

But her mother were nowt as Nast

When it come to looks and nice nature

Her mother woulda come in last

Yin Yang and me needed to be alone

I'd got fit and spent three weeks Ont wagon

We found a place where we hoped she'd not find us

First kiss, then Enter the Dragon!

Mary liked us going fishing

But she couldn't shut up bloody talkin

I said you need to keep quiet

As down to the boat we were walk-in

Me mum and dad are coming with us too

Shark fishin wit parents in laws!

We'll need a bigger boat and sound proofing

Noisy buggers, jaws, jaws and jaws.

60.

St Thomas's Social club.

Nowt special about an owd building,

Down a street in a hard part of town.

But it's better than sittin at home,

When nowt on telly is the only sound.

Nowt special about a few pals,

Chewin't cud and having a laugh.

Abawt Tommy wakin up freezin cowd

When he'd fawn asleep in the bath.

(chorus)

Well Billy plays guitar and Jimmy talks abawt war,

Then we all sing songs of freedom,

At St Thomas's Social club.

Mavis makes the brews, keeps goin on an on abawt news.

Now there's an empty chair or two

At St Thomas's Social club.

John sucks on't pipe an invisible blend,

Cos there's nothin burnin at business end.

He plays dominoes wi a poker face,

And he's ten bob richer when he leaves the place.

Mary and Maude get up fert dance,

They'd prefer a bloke, but they've got no chance.

I'd rather hear Billy singin't blues,

Now me feet can't drive me dancin shoes.

Three times a week in that bare back room,

But its a world apart from the outside gloom.

Nowt on offer these days much to me likin,

But that's just me and there's no use skrikin.

A sort of brotherhood a sort of clan,

I woulda thought it nowt as a younger man.

Feeytin off injuns with a bowie knife,

Now I'm in the fading streets of later life.

61.

Today is national Haiku day. Haiku has three lines, the first and last have five syllables and the middle seven. Here is my offering.

Haiku rules are strict

You need to be concise or

You will run out of

62.

It was good being an altar boy at Sacred Heart

You felt special in your cassock and your cotta

Especially as an Acolyte carrying the big candle

Or the Thurifer with thurible burning incense

Part of something outside of the ordinary

With sunlight split in colours through the stained glass

The Tabernacle light meant God was inside

The statues and the Stations of the Cross

The Latin Mass sung magically chanting

The Sanctus bells at Transubstantiation

Part of some great historic mystery

That overshed the point of life outside

I remember one morning just before Christmas

With bells and incense, congregation overflowing

The choir sweetly singing Agnus Dei

When I spied outside the sky had started snowing

Then deep inside with no church rules demanding

I felt a true peace with no understanding.

63.

Flies are hard faced

They have no manners at all

They come in uninvited

Then taunt you on the wall

You get your rolled up paper

Approach with stealth and skill

With a swooping arc perfectly aimed

You close in for the kill

Then, as if by magic

The fat little git disappears

Then you notice the holes in the floorboards

Confirming your worst fears

Woodworm are cheeky bastards

We finally got rid of the mouse

Then woodworm come a calling

"Do you mind if we eat your house!"

64.

Art awreet? Ahm awreet, wharever awreet means.

Ups and deawns an ins an eawts and all the in betweens.

Mi 'eds inside mi trilby and mi feet are in mi shoes.

Ahm awreet and they't awreet and tharrel haf fert do.

I seed an owd pal the other day when I were walking.

He said neaw av not seen thee for a while.

Not much gooin on we started talkin

Carried on wi walkin for a mile.

Last time I seed thee, theay were on fire.

Waitin for thi wench eawtside o't 'Sheaf.

Theay sed it then an I thowt theay were a liar

Tha said "make the most o this cos time's a thief".

I think her's gooin funny keeps sayin everything twice

Her made me prato pie for tea and that were nice

I'm thinkin o gooin into politics, eether that or breedin carp

Sort them daft buggers eawt in London, before I go up playin't th'arp.

65.

I was busking in Bergerac

Under the statue of the big nosed duelist

Hat in his hand, gazing at the sky

A woman hung her towels from an upstairs window

Another shouted to her and they laughed in French

Cobbled walkways down to the wide Dordogne

Fat boats bobbing in chains

Locals walking past in their world

The guitar echoing in the alleyways

A waiter polishing a wine glass

Making places for four on the white linen

I was there but I was not there

An outsider with a mask of music

Fingers blue in the chilly shadow of Cyrano

66.

Just found an old boat in the garden

It were hiding behind some weeds

I can sail it to Preston Marina

I know a bloke theer called Steve

He'll fix it up reet and proper

Then we'll get charts out and see

How fert sail from Preston to Bali

Some ship shape shape shifters and me.

67.

In a northern town down a cobbled street

In a smoky pub where the old pals meet

When it's opening time and the lights are shining

So every storm cloud has a silver lining

Brass bar gleams and the optics glitter

Two bob ont bar for a pint of bitter

Pat ont back and a jovial greeting

Light fert cig in that moment fleeting

A little time to pick up life's strands

After't days hard graft wi leather hands

Not much to say, not much to think

Just concentrate on t'day's first drink

Look up at light through t'bottom o't glass

Like owd George said All things must pass.

68.

What is this Progressive Elsie?

Is it like rock music and eating frogs?

No Mary it's not that, it's letting

Grown men go into women's bogs.

Why would they want that Elsie?

It's forward thinking and it's new

Like teaching little children about anal sex

They've started doing that too.

They know what they're doing Elsie

They're clever and it's a brand new world.

I know and I'm probably wrong but

They should just let them be boys and girls.

We're what you call fascists now Elsie

You know them that stick up their fists.

And the biggest threat to society are

Not the progressives, No it's the Methodists!

69.

They said she was wrong, she was ridiculed

Unfriended, unloved, what an awkward bitch

She went against all the rules and advice

Burn the witch

She would not conform, she would not shut up

She was shunned, a foregone conclusion

The others would huddle in little tight groups

Reconfirming each others delusion

But oh there's a reward not being part of the crowd

Not being their version of you to comply

You wake up free, you go to sleep free

Free till the day you die.

Not worrying a bit what the in crowd think

It confuses them, removes their power

They really wanted to burn the witch

A free, beautiful, unfake wild flower.

70.

The Rucks.

I broke my coccyx sliding down Hart Common rucks on a piece of corrugated tin.

I encountered a kind of ski jump and what goes up comes down agin.

Black Alps to us carved in rainy rivulets and crumbling cliffs falls.

Some still smoking after decades through volcano holes in the walls

Gyproc rucks were red, like a crumbling rusty smokey Matterhorn

Plenty of my knee blood on them crags the crimson dust to join

I still cawnt sit up properly due to that lower spine misdemeanour

Maybe if we'd had climbing ropes, some sense and some carabiner

The coal spoil black and shiny, they took it all fert level t'motorways

I can still see the sun glinting off the sides at the end of a mystery day

Piles of slag or piles of gold, childhood memories, I'll get o'er um.

Our Black Alps, Himalyayas, Church street Andes, Karakorum.

71.

He lived on 12 o clock hill

Huge slabs of mist joined together and formed a thin sea

He ate breakfast above it in the sunshine

Below the mist people banged against each other and argued

He could hear the cacophony through his ear trumpet

While he smoked a cheroot and dreamed

Dreams of a free noble life

Where everyone was nice and honest and humble

Where they lived like Jesus and the church was the street

Where all the animals trusted us

People didn't try to control other people

Kindness was universal and natural

And happiness spread like a sine curve

In lustrous shallow waves across the world.

72.Central heating engineer explaining boilers

He had condensing Combi on his lips

Next thing he's being chased by a dead man

Oh no! Zombie Apocalypse.

Models on the catwalk wearing casual clothes

Abercrombie Fitch with zips

Suddenly they're dripping blood and screaming

Yet another Zombie Apocalypse

Lady A or Mom B, what to wear, what to eat?

He chose Mom B, a frock and chips

Little did he know she was an undead

Here we go Zombie Apocalypse

Dining in the new fast French food cafe

She ordered pommes frites, a choc and dips

Waiter's eyes transform into blackness

Yikes its a Zombie Apocalypse

Another night on my own watching telly

Enjoying Sitcom, tea, a wok o crisps

There's a knocking sound on the window

Yes you know Zombie Apocalypse!

73.

All the newspaper men told us

So did the BBC

To all the intelligent, learned ones it was very plain to see

All the professors and the doctors and the politicians too

Gasped in admiration at the Emperor's clothes so new

They must have cost a fortune, the tailors were the best

Made in secret behind closed doors, we are so very blessed

To witness such craftsmanship that stands us all in awe

Their plans were so meticulous without a single flaw

Millions accepted the perfect scene they gazed upon

Till a little boy said "Mummy, why has that man got nothing on"

74.

New daft poem for today IMPOSSIBLE me and Lawrence Hoy were discussing.

Some words are impossible to rhyme

Readers Digest said like "wolf"

Depends on your pronunciation

North and south is a bit of a gulf.

Then the next word they said is impossible

That famous non-rhymer "orange"

But if you come from owd Westhoughton

Everyone knows Jimmy Gorringe.

One more impossible rhymer

Number three on the list was "woman"

I know lots of intelligent ladies

But I'm sure here and there there's a dumb un.

I'm making em up as I'm going along

Number four impossible is "husband"

But when you pay money on public transport

You could stretch it a bit to a bus fund.

Number five got me thinking

No word can rhyme with "purple"

But it reminded me of working ont farm

With me owd mate Kevin Purtill

If you're not too strict with grammar

And pronunciation and poetic practices

You can make up rhymes for anything

Like pulling pricks off cactuses.

75.

Just watched an American violent film

True to life it said, that's rich

Bloke had both his legs blown off

And he shouted Son of a bitch!

Another bloke escaping from a burning plane

Encountered a bit of a hitch

Parachute failed to open

And he shouted Son of Bitch!

Villain trapped in his crashed car

Seatbelt suffered a bit of a glitch

Petrol tank exploded

And he murmured Son of a bitch!

One came home from a boozy night

In the kitchen hit the light switch

His wife had left gas cooker on

Explosion! Son of a bitch!

One mon hanging by his fingertips

Too scared to even twitch

Seagull starts pecking his eyes out

He shouted Son of a bitch!

Just as film reached its climax

Hero looking dead in a ditch

Does he survive? Telly blew up,

I thowt Son of a bitch!

76.

The Goodies.

We used to be the goodies

We used to wipe the floor

With all the baddies and the nasties

We're not the goodies anymore.

Maybe we were just the bullies

When we held our flags aloft

After beating all the foreigners

But now the West's gone soft

Gone perverted, gone corrupted

Full of calories and phlegm

Not the fighters and the workers

No I don't mean them

I mean the career politicians

The progressives, the elite

Who never had a job

Who never slept cold in a street

Who lecture us on morals

Try to show us their new ways

While all the strength and all the honour

Shrinks with all the passing days

They still think they are the winners

Sitting there with flags unfurled

In their nasty little gatherings

Think they can lecture all the world

But the world is passing by them

Nobody needs them anymore

From the little Indian farmer

To the Chinese stevedore

They don't want old drunken westerners

Bragging what they're going to do

They've moved on to greener pastures

No longer need red, white and blue.

77.

The Boneworks.

Piles of intestines int corner

Stomachs and lungs in another

Bones and brains and eyes

Looking dead straight at each other

Horns and hooves and jawbones

Blanchin' ont concrete int th'heat

Watch where you're searching for maggots

Wi blood and fat stuck to your feet

Got maggots neaw we go fishing

Trampin' across Howfen lands

Cast in then reach for me butties

Never mind washin' mi hands.

Boneworks once mashed up an elephant

Dropped off from Chester Zoo

That must have made massive maggots

Woulda tempted a big perch or two.

A posh bloke from Oxford came't Wingates

He were sat int th'Horsehoe on a cheer

Said he'd a meeting at Burns' Boneworks

Tom said "Don't tell me they're gettin' smell deawn theer!"

78.

Gone - x

Horseshoe is gone, Wigglesworths is gone

Boneworks is gone, Cross Guns is gone

Windmill is gone, Starkie is flats

Metal Box gone, just houses and cats

De Havilland's gone, Red Lion's a home

All of the streetscapes gone monochrome

Most of the churches most of the pubs

Gone for the streets full of houses and shrubs

Clouds still push over Rivi from't West

Rain still doing what rain does best

All the best songs have been written

All the best sayings have been said

All the best men and the ladies

Gone to their permanent bed

Somehow I'm still here on licence

Been spared for a brave new day

Lucky I know, like the living

Funny things turn out that way

So I better not waste this new moment

While mi body and brain are not jelly

No sitting ont couch and rotting

Watching brainwashing shite on the telly

Out in the wind in mi rags

Out in the pure blessed rain

What's gone is gone and that's history

And we'll see nowt like it again.

79.

15 Minute City.

Everything you need is in the 15 minute city

Entertainment, work, food, home and life

All the techno dreamworlds rolled into one

Protected from the outside world of strife

Tidy lustrous walkways, clean filtered air

Hospitals and schools contained within

All will be delivered, no need for you to cook

Yes and churches to confess your little sin

We have thought of everything the human spirit wants

Comfort, warmth, exercise and fun

Safety, co-existence with your fellow man

Real rain, real thunder, real sun

She walked out through the gates and past the goonsquad guards

She wandered past the outskirts of the town

She found the little stream and she followed it for miles

She came to a quiet corner and lay down

A dragonfly buzzed closely, landed on her foot

A little bird looked at her from a tree

In the distance was the hulk of the 15 minute city

Shimmering glass reflecting reality

She felt free and she felt dirty

She lay there cold and hungry in the night

Everything you need is in the 15 minute city

Nearly everything but not quite.

80.

Song for today - Perfect.

She had ice blue sparkling eyes, she was a little overweight

Her laugh could twinklify the room, her teeth weren't geometric straight.

She'd never hurt a living thing and she was almost alway late

She didn't sneer or turn him down when he asked her for a date

She was perfect.

He didn't look like that Brad Pitt and he worked on building sites

He like a few pints with his pals but he'd never start a fight

When she spoke he tried to listen but he didn't always get it

But he was soft with her kitten, when it bit him he would let it

He was perfect

The night was cold, the night was dark it started drizzling in the town

His car kept stalling, spluttering. Cafe looked a bit run down

But the fire was burning bright and the food was cheap and good

Their chatter silly, embarrassing, first awkward kiss blazed his blood

It was perfect.

81.

The Corridor.

As he aged the corridor grew thinner

Made from past choices and a wasteful seeping

Cheap thrills sought, time squandered

No seeds sown for future reaping

When it came too thin to pass

And old ways lost what edge they had

A rusty heavy useless knife

To kill a life already dead

Then at rock bottom came the spark

And from the spark began rebirth

An inner change, a higher power

To give, at last, his life some noble worth

Then the corridor could be seen

For what it was, a self made fiction

There never was a corridor

But that created by his addiction

82.

Misdirection. (New protest song for today)

She's flashing her knickers but he's got a gun

Hitchiking outside a bar

You're concentrating on the wrong one

For God's sake don't stop the car.

Misdirection is a magic trick

To make you look the wrong way

That's why you always need to look behind

The words that politicians say

Female Brown Trout fake orgasm

To ditch their current date

She makes him feel good about himself

While she welcomes in a new mate

Tony Blair wants digital ID's

So they'll know who has been jabbed

This is to protect you my friend

Meanwhile your back's being stabbed

Some snakes pretend to be venomous

To keep the killers at bay

Bright red stripes, the predator flees

Soft snake has a good day

Misdirection is a magic trick

To make you look the wrong way

That's why you always need to look behind

The words that politicians say

The Peewit pretends to have a broken wing

And flutters off round the field

There's nothing wrong with her of course

But she keeps her nest of chicks concealed

Fauci stands with a scowl on his face

He worked so hard for the cause

His bank balance grew by 10 million bucks

And now he wants the applause

So if you want to find the Peewits eggs

Ignore her deceitful dash

To find political reasons

Its apt to follow the cash

Misdirection is a magic trick

To make you look the wrong way

That's why you always need to look behind

The words that politicians say

83.

Thoughts on Women's Day.

I like women, they're funny.

Me mother was one and so's me wife

They come from a different planet

But without them on earth, no life

They see things that I don't

Like on shelves and hiding int fridge

And they give me ignored advice

Like when I jumped off the Iron Bridge

They look nice and soft and shiny

And most of them are cleaner than me

They can do lots of things that I can't

And they make more imaginative tea

Most of them are rubbish at violence

And can't keep up with me on a bender

But all in all, weighing up facts

They're a pretty acceptable gender.

84.

Question everything you are confronted by lies,

Look after your children, never fear.

The ordinary man in the street will never die,

Don't wait for the future it is here.

They're fighting in the streets fang and tooth

Hitting baseball bats like Babe Ruth

We would just like to be told the true truth

Why am I yelling? - what are you selling?

Question everything they want your digital ID

Their cameras follow every move you make

They'll take away your cash, jab your arm and scan your eyes

Squeeze each ounce of courage till you break.

Money elites own the media and the banks and the tanks

That little group of people pull the strings

Proxy wars and proxy science, cultural removal

Rewrite history, burn your wedding rings.

Hello Mr Blair, Mr Soros, Mr Schwab

What hateful plans you working on today

15 minutes cities, digital implants, doctored news

Are little people getting in your way?

They wrap it up in fake morality

We'll save your life, save your planet, just agree

Cos everything is done on their terms

taking poison, eating beetles, eating worms.

Question everything, burn all newspapers now,

Throw a big brick through your new TV.

Yellow vest are visible, the bankers are invisible,

The rulers never want you to be free.

Question everything, but don't fall in hate,

Love your fellow man from all the earth.

Why is all the money in the hands of the few,

Its getting worse, its getting worse, its getting worse.

85.

Ministry of Truth.

You're either working for your fellow man or you're working for the Ministry.

No half way measures any more they've shown their hand you see.

No use waiting for Labour, Labour isn't labour anymore

They stopped being Labour when they showed old Jeremy the door

We need defiance not compliance, we need to stick together to be free.

You're either working for your fellow man or you're working for the Ministry.

Funny how all the western governments now singing the same new tunes

Moral guardians of truth backed by their black clad goons

They become stronger and they need for us to fight one another

Agreeing with their rules and reporting your sister or your brother

But we need to stick together and we need everyone to see

You're either working for your fellow man or you're working for the Ministry.

May seem like nothing to worry about but things are changing really fast

Move the power to the globalists and your take for granted freedoms won't last

They signed a treaty with the W.H.O like Pontius Pilate they can wash their hands

Force their digital ID's and vaccine mandates and lockdowns from faraway lands

It's for your own good they say, the greater good of all humanity

You're either working for your fellow man or you're working for the Ministry.

War and Woke and Trans and BLM are just distractions for their greater good

They're so confident they filled each western government with their blood

Its been a long road for them but its coming to conclusion soon

And we need to be ready or we will all be singing their same tune

Did you notice when they were laying down their laws their faces were full of glee

You're either working for your fellow man or you're working for the Ministry.

You know when people kill themselves it's little things that make the final straw

Losing all the things you took for granted is life worth living any more

Their disastrous mistakes or things they do on purpose to control you

There will be no come backs for them they are above the law, rules are just for you

Old lady in her house alone in silence as the sun sets on what used to be

You're either working for your fellow man or you're working for the Ministry.

86.

Bobby.

The pavement was hard but the coffee was gold

A jet left its sign in the sky pushing west.

The layers of coats couldn't keep out the cold.

But the steam from the cup! and the smile did the rest.

Venus is twinkling as the morning star rose,

On Bobby and me my little fourlegged satnav.

You sleep in my jacket, you eat from my hands.

Don't die tonight Bobby you're all that I have.

Each town has the concrete, each town has the rain.

The doorways are few and they're all taken up.

But Bobby and me we'll find solace tonight.

A bottle for me, biscuits in his paper cup.

We're in today Bobby she just gave me a note.

Special biscuits for you and the usual for me.

It'll be different tomorrow, we'll start something new.

Come on Bobby just you wait and see.

87.

What is behind the shades of the black clad goon paid to carry out the wishes of the elite.

For money he is willing to use violence to keep the ordinary people off the street.

He doesn't have a name or a number, he doesn't have compassion in his soul.

He's big and he's hard and his brain is ticking slowly inside a biological black hole.

What is behind the shades of a man who is willing to do the master's dirty work.

Does he go home to a wife and a family in what dismal streets does he lurk.

Can money be enough to turn off the guilt, turn off the wrong and right and the shame

Who created such creatures, traitorous and cold, who really should accept the blame.

Well it starts with saying nothing, just nodding and agreeing, go along with everything they say.

Don't think too much about the implications, not your problem and you've had a busy day.

One thing leading to another, subtle changes become less subtle after time.

What is behind the shades of the black clad goons? Us when we stand in line.

88.

There is a rat in my mind

Keeps biting nerve ends once seemed dead

And lights up streets of memory

With little alleys glowing in new thoughts

At twelve minutes past two

It bites my sleep

As I swim in darkness deep

Then I wonder where I am in a world of trouble

It is a nice rat as rats go

Without it I wouldn't grow

And just drift along choose not to know

How lucky to be alive

A unique, fresh moment, ungravitised in the cosmos.

89.

Jackson Pollock.

Jackson Pollock dropped a bollock carrying paint through his studio door.

Oils and thinners, multiple colours, crashed down to the concrete floor.

Streaks and dollops, drips and slashes, purple, yellow and blue.

"I give up!" Cried Jackson desperately, "I just don't know what to do".

"This Art job is a disaster, there is just no money in it."

Then he looked at the tangled mess on the floor and thought "Hey just a minute…"

90. The poem that your software just deleted

I didn't mean it literally you know?

Its called irony do you allow that?

Computer says no.

I'll be able to buy things using cash yes?

I like to use cash wherever I go

How and what I spend is my own business.

Computer says no.

That yellow camera that just got me driving past

I wasn't driving fast I was rather slow

Surely I can drive down this road without paying?

Computer says no.

I don't want to key all my details in.

You don't need my life story blow by blow

I don't want to give up all my privacy like that

Computer says no.

Is this an indication of the future?

I need fingerprints and digital photo

Can't I just get by as a free independent man?

Computer says no.

91.

Listen to the bullshit of the mainstream news

Settle in a comfy chair

Ignore the strangled voices with their different views

Just pretend that they're not there.

Buy the propaganda fake morality

Be sure to contribute when you are told

Never stray across their line of right and wrong

Ignore the homeless beggar in the cold

Don't try to be too analytical

You don't want to be left there on the shelf

Much better to be in the middle of the crowd

So stop that thinking for yourself

All you need to know is on the BBC

They lay it out so simple and so true

After all they wouldn't have an axe to grind

You pay the licence so they work for you.

92.

H

Ahm 'appy , 'ealthy and 'armless

'onest', 'umble and sometimes 'ilarious

On bad days ahm 'orrid, 'ideous and 'ostile

'ateful, 'aughty and even 'ebetudinous

But I try to be 'elpful, I try to be 'ospitable

'ygenic, 'onorable, and not too 'yperbolic

I knew someone who pronounced his aitches proper

Words like hawesome, hadept and halcoholic.

93.

I squeezed the last drop of electricity from the national grid

As the radio crackled into silence

They said only 15 minutes left until the end of the world

Cities erupting in looting, rape and violence

An explosive armageddon on route from space

Could not be diverted from its line

May as well go up to the top of the hill

To watch the asteroid coming in on time

They said few who might survive like zombies from hell

Would desecrate all memories in their path

So I torched the house and all our possessions

Leaving nothing to the loveless psycopaths

The house and car ablaze as I topped the little hill

And there the black colossus in the sky!

Approaching at sixty thousand miles an hour

I lit a cig and waited there to die

As the sky darkened and the end was nigh

I flicked that Park Drive butt into its face

And wonder of wonders that little extra force of physics

Caused the asteroid to veer off into space!

Who would have thought that smoking a cig

Could have saved the world and everybody in it.

Now I could return to my lovely pleasant home

There's a smell of smoke, oh just a bloody minute…

94.

New song - Another Dream Day is Gone.

Went for a walk on the white glistening lane

A bitter wind stung from the east

Hands in mi pockets, scarf round mi neck

Looked like a Mongolian beast

Thanks nature god for this mystery day

For me to do with what I will

From the edge of the ridge I could see the white walls

Of the snow covered Winter Hill

It passes so quickly and dies with the sun

Another dream day will be gone.

Lucky am I to be living this day

When so many others have gone

Grey sheen of Ribble strides the north sky

No-one here but I'm never alone

Sheep on the hillside, birds in the air

Oak, Ash and Holly abound

There it sets off in the wink of an eye

Free hare disturbed by my sound.

It passes so quickly and dies with the sun

Another dream day will be gone.

There is a fierce free world up in the trees

Where the wind shakes a rising of birds

I can smell the outside scent on mi clothes

I can't put that affection in words

Sluggish the stream as the far water slides

Between the black walls of slutch

All the green things waiting in cold hesitating

For life but it won't take that much

It passes so quickly and it dies with the sun

Another dream day will be gone.

95.

New Song - Carol Vorderman's t***.

They're building mRNA jab factories around the world.

Investing so much money in your health

Meanwhile in Davos they're constructing your future

Only expertise needed there is wealth

Millions are starving in Yemen,

While Kissinger's trying to start world war three

But according to the Daily Star, the biggest news by far

Carl Vorderman's bust is now 34D.

Over 200,000 homeless in uk today

That is dwarfed by numbers around the world

People can't afford to heat their homes

Meanwhile more war banners unfurled

Hospitals are full and churches empty

Leader of the free world still alive, but only just.

Yet according to the Daily Star, the biggest news by far

Carol's arse is now less famous than her bust.

They're trying to make it illegal to demonstrate

If you defame the government you could end up inside

Truth is lies and lies are truth

All the western leaders with the media on their side.

Get rid of jobs we have artificial intelligence

Annually we lose ten billion trees

The oceans are full of masks and plastic

How long would we live without the bees

Mainstream news and lockdowns maintained fear

People pay for it to scare themselves to bits

But the biggest news by far, according to the Daily Star

Look at the size of Carol Vorderman's ****.

96.

Its theer.

Wheer?

Theer!

I cawnt see it.

Near yon sheep.

What sheep?

Theer!

Wheer?

Ah! neaw ah con see it.

Now not that, that!

What?

That!

Wheer?

THEER!

97.

Who shall I believe today

The one with the cheque book and grin

Or the one who stands to lose everything

Those with the power and media on side

Or those who risk ridicule for not having lied.

Truth, lies and statistics

We are bombarded all waking hours

But only truth needs no money or spin

So often discarded and thrown in the bin

Ignored in the weeds and the flowers

Straight faced liars sure know how to spin it.

Honest truth? There's just no money in it.

98.

New year, new brain. (New song for today)

New year new brain, thowd one were insane,

So I chucked it out, New one cost nowt.

Each sploshing step, down the rainy lane

Gives me a chance to try out mi new brain.

There's a spudger in the sky and it's looking happy,

Cos it cares not one jot for the pain of man.

And a cheeky daffodil just stuck its yed out

Each year gives it a chance to start again.

Mud half way up mi leg, this path's well trodden,

Then it comes to a bridge wi pebbles and a twinklin stream.

Funny how rain and gravity create such beauty,

New brain thinks its livin in a dream.

Fourteen escaped pheasants live wi me now,

Them heroes wi shotuns won't kill thee toneet.

Tha can have some corn and I'll just sit and watch thi,

New brain can watch nowt and its still a treat

Black the sky is looming dotted wi diamonds,

They exist a million years in the past.

To them I'm just an atom livin on an atom,

99.

Don't conform, do not comply.

They think nothing of you

Your health and happiness is immaterial to them

You are a million ones to the right of the decimal point

To the Megas, the Smarts, the Elites.

Be the one who stands when others kneel

Block the Media, block the news

Walk in the fields and love the sky

Do not be afraid, they want you to be afraid,

They smile and laugh, they are so confident.

They are few and they own so much

They own The Science

But they don't own science.

They own the Media

But they don't own truth.

They fashion The Future

But they don't own the future.

Be true to your family and friends

Have courage to change the things you can.

100.

Sorry!

It were quiet int club when this big bloke

Spilt his pint all over mi aunty Florrie

She's a mannerly wench and she looked at him drenched

Then she said that old English word Sorry!

I were walkin cross car park in Tescos

When he run oer mi foot in his lorry

I were writhin ont floor but I knocked ont cab door

And shouted that English word Sorry!

I were collectin fossils right peaceful

When he dropped a rock on mi head from top o't quarry

Before I sunk into't slime I still made the time

To utter that English word Sorry!

But I found him int British Legion

Watchin Monday's edition of Corrie

With mi shotgun blast I geet revenge at last

Just in time to hear him say Sorry!

101.

Sometimes I think I'm Irish.

I feel Irish somehow.

The mood and walking in the green rain

The music stirrin deep within

Like being somewhere again and again

Maybe they wouldn't have me

It wouldn't matter anyhow

Cos I know deep down I'm Irish

In Killarney with me fiddle and me cow

Gazing west oer vast Atlantic

Listenin' to blarney in the bars

I can talk shite and love deep

But mi fightin power's underpar

I could work on that and the Guinness

I could work like I used to ont sites

I'd be alright alone and Irish

Wandrin' home as old age bites.

102.

Black and white landscape calmly assaults my eyesight.

I was called to come here by the spirits of the night.

Met the ice queen in the hill snow forest bliss,

Smoke floats off her cheek from my evaporating kiss.

A volley of shotgun fire, did not see her go,

Not a single footprint to be seen in the snow.

They killed the poor pheasant just trying to feed

They killed our liaison what a dastardly deed!

103.

Snow isn't impressed by the Left or the Right,

When it floats down unhindered in the dark basalt night,

The wind can't be bought or persuaded by greed,

No flattery, backhanders can alter its speed.

The media can't paint the red sunset blue

It is what it is, takes no notice of you.

While experts and scientists make computer projections,

Nature at ease creates simple perfections.

That make all our creations seem petty and cheap,

When it transforms the landscape while we are asleep.

When it booms from volcanoes its sulphurous fires

And a brave little Robin shows most humans as liars.

104.

Murdered bird.

Purest clear light creating a little warmth

Under the still trees in early December

Black spindly silhouettes reach out

To catch its fragile gift

As tiny birds eager for its rays

Busy feeding while they can.

One ripped bloody in an instant

Another feeder feasts warm meat

In the cold truth of nature

Seen by my human freak brain

Such beautiful perfect forms

Such beautiful horror.

105.

I find pontificating moralists the most hateful

Preaching diverse love and self flagellation

Telling poor working class whites to be grateful

Being born with the privilige of this colonist nation

Your ancesters working in factories, mills and pits

Average life expectancy no better than slaves

While the owners and bankers, politicians and spivs

Grew wealthier by the growth of their penniless graves

They're still at it jetting around and drinking champagne

On the TV explaining to the bloke from Platt Bridge

You're so lucky to be born in this country, give more

As he turns off the heating and scrats round his fridge

Get off your high horses you gas guzzling gits

North London elite, globalist bankers

Millionaire sportsmen, children of Lords

Career politicians, TV show anchors.

(TV show anchors is my new rhyming slang)

106.

Today's connections.

My computer is connected to my windmill

Only working when the breeze is in the west

When I'm inspired and the wind is misdirecting

I have to write on paper, its the best.

I've converted my car to run on wood fire

Huge flames boil the water then the steam

Drives pistons in the boot, the wheels connected

As long as I have logs, runs like a dream

My dreams a vivid abstract of reality

I awake sometimes at three with a jerk

My heart connects its morals to my brain

If I had a soul it would make the whole thing work.

107.

Trying to help in The Asda

As she bent over the frozen food section

The sight of her caused an awkward inflection

In my voice. She was choosing her favourite tipples

Standing proud in the coldness her raspberry ripples

I was holding my sauce hollandaise

When she intercepted my gaze

She dropped three packs of gum, a bottle of rum,

So I made a quick grab for her two tins of chum

I was out of my wits

As she near did the splits

I tried to assist taking hold of her bits

That fell on the shiny new floor

Before security threw me out of the door?

Why?

108. Alexa are you there, Do you care, I would like to share

Play me a melody that used to be part of a different life.

Alexa Play me some blues, Disconnect the news, Order me some booze

Play me a melody that used to be part of a different life.

I went up Rivi and the coastline seemed in reach,

But in my brain I've always had a splinter.

For 30 miles the Lancashire plain seemed fast asleep,

As the west sky faded into Winter

Alexa what is it that I lack, Please rub my back, I've give myself the sack.

Play me a melody that used to be part of a different life.

Alexa where's my drink, I'm on the brink, Give me time to think.

Play me a melody that used to be part of a different life.

I'm too tight to put the heating on tonight.

I think I'll leave it till December.

I used to fly, I used to run, I used to love,

Buy Christmas presents in November.

Alexa make me laugh, Can you fix that draught, Say something daft

Play me a melody that used to be part of a different life.

109.

Lord Snooty loved the taste of London Gin

"From the city" he said, nothing could be finer.

But when he looked on the table

On the bottle, on the label, the fatal words

Made in China.

Hank liked his American line dancing boots.

He bought them in a store, North Carolina

Sliding them on in his den

He saw aghast besides "Size 10" the fatal words

Made in China.

When the iceberg saw the end of the Titanic

British shipbuilding went down with that great liner.

But as icy water sealed its fate

In small letters on the nameplate, the fatal words

Made in China.

Mavis was frustrated with her sex life

It wasn't helped by her acute angina

In a "Private Shop" in Paris

She bought the toy, a bit embarrassed

When she opened it said: Made in China!

110.

Sometimes something comes along

That's just better than all the rest

Maybe a performance or a song

But it surpasses every test

For that moment, for that time

It stands alone, a fragile thing

Almost perfect yet still fragile

For at its birth its death bells ring

Others come to take it

Try and change it to their own

Dress it up and make it complex

Put it on a tinsel throne

Then the fickle people fumble

In the dark for something new

And forget that glorious moment

When that something shone so true

111.

Messy Peas for Disaster.

Take a tin of exasperated milk

Three strange eggs and

Some selfish raisin flour.

Then a rarer sugar

Steal some salt and pepper

Put it int fridge for an hour.

Get a bit of dry white swine

Dip it in helicopter flower

Some egg fly lice

And two festive sugar rats

Eat it under Blackpool tower.

112.

My New French Song.

I want to write a French song maybe a Belgian song

With a bit of Italian and Spanish thrown in.

I must pay homage to my European pals

Put down this chip butty and adjust my accent to sing.

Wandering down the Champs Elysees along the

Leeds and Liverpool canal in the rain

I left my heart in San Francisco, no Santiago,

No Lower Ince no South Dordogne in Eymet.

I'm living in a French film noir tragi-comedy

Wearing a blue and white hooped shirt and a black beret.

My long moustache is curled and so is my nose

As round my neck I have a string of onions Ok.

The crack of a pistol someone is shot

Down a back alley they got him in the chest.

Pity he didn't have an escape bicycle and

A fashionable Christian Dior bullet proof vest.

I've taken some tranquilizers mixed with viagra

It's a french trick taking this mystery drug.

It makes you randy but if nobody fancies you

And you don't get any You just give a gallic shrug.

I need to change my appearance dye my hair black

And greasy with a central parting.

Please send me some Euros and some fancy Italian

Leather zip up boots to replace these old Doc Martens.

I'm running out of ideas think I'll get some

Cognac a croissant and just lie on my back.

Is that Blackpool through the fog or the Eiffel tower

I'm in a dead end what's french for cul-de-sac?

113.

It costs a fortune to use the hoover these days,

Washing machine! don't even think of the tumble dryer.

Hot water in the sink, boiling kettle for a drink,

Cooking food int microwave and air fryer.

DIY, using power tools, wasting juice,

Then the ironing, read the electric meter ouch!

Because I care and I want to save the planet

I'll be here all day unconscious on the couch.

114.

He couldn't see the beauty of the little hilltop village

The old stone houses and the winding cobbled bliss.

He didn't feel the peace of the covered cooling walkways

He could only think where is the drink in this.

All the places he'd been told to visit by his friends

Seemed lacking compared to their defining.

The only thing that stirred his heart when he found it

Was the tavern with the neon beer light shining.

Every picture, every town, every famous beauty spot

Statues, fountains, pretty squares entwining.

Faded and folded underneath his dark desire

To see the tavern with the neon beer light shining.

Nothing really matters or stirs his weary soul

He's seen it all and he couldn't be impressed

Cold and golden in his hand here at last was something grand

The glass that held the answers to his quest.

115.

Today is the last day of summer and tomorrow autumn begins.

So I went for a walk in the evening sunshine to the top of the hill for my sins.

I could see right over past Pendle, into Yorkshire and up to the Lakes

Not a sight or a sound of a human sat ont bench to confront my mistakes

But like August the past is receding and in time we will all be replaced

So I let that sun's warmth melt mi memories and shine on mi wrinkly face

God grant me the peace and serenity and health that I may not deserve

But I'll take it and what I do with it will depend on the masters I serve

So for masters I'll choose them more wisely than maybe I have done before

And look forward to each daily blessing as we open up future's front door.

116.

Raindrops don't lie, trees don't lie,

Humans lie

And the more powerful the person the bigger the lie

Don't be too quick to nail your flag to a mast

Political parties, all of them, lie

Big organisations, all of them, lie

Big media lies

So where is the truth?

It is hard to find, it takes time and work and courage.

Listen to the ones who have most to lose

The ones who are not paid by the Big

Listen to the ones who know they will be vilified

For speaking out and for being one in a million

The outsiders, not in the mainstream

The ones who speak truth because it is true

Not because it is useful

Truth is simple

Like the raindrop and the tree.

117.

Forged the copper Brussels sprouts

Fried in mercury in a tungsten pan

Blobbed them out with fat lead spuds

And served them to the iron man

Through his glass fronted stomach

And down his plastic throat

You could see the chemical digestion

Through the slits in his silver coat

I wandered off to the river

Realising I was made of meat

Awful offal in my core

Rotten flesh from head to feet

Through eyes of gin clear jelly

Sending visions to my grey sludge brain

The dreams, the dreams, the too real dreams!

Haunting sleep's dawn shores again.

118.

Just seed a woman crossin't road

Wi loads o shoppin' bags, on't phone to her Mam

Un three little dogs on't leads un pushin't babby in her pram

Wi no free hand visible her managed leet a cig as well

Talk abeawt multi-taskin' a thowt bloody hell!

(True story, just seen in Eccleston)

119.

Trickle, trinkle, plip, plop, ploop

Soil is drinking nature's soup

Drizzle, mizzle, scattering rain

Trees are glowing green again

Drenching, quenching sating thirst

Little dams of ditch dust burst

Birdies dipping, feathers shivering

Streams streaming, rivers rivering

Hold the brimming cup aloft

Lancashire water, sweet and soft.

120.

New song - Little Blue Shoes.

A box full of nothing important

Along with the rest bound for't tip

Carried it out from the boot of my car

Balanced one side on my hip

Looked through the rags and the papers

Dusty books, old clothes and old news

And there at the bottom, scuffed and curled up

Her first pair of little blue shoes.

(chorus)

They both fit in my hand very easy

Hard to think, such small feet, tiny toes

But they can still tell a tale of patience and love

For that little thing so long ago.

They are no use to anybody

They come from a different day

Describing a time that seems so long ago

Now she's grown and she's flown away

Scuffed from her first tries at walking

The laughter the falls and the tears

Do they end up in the skip with the rest of the junk

Forgotten for so many years.

No use being too sentimental

No room in the house for this stuff

I need to make space for some new things

Old things we've more than enough.

Threw the box in the skip and departed

Made me mind up, nothing to lose

But there on the passenger seat by my side

Her first pair of little blue shoes.

121.

These little shoes are no use anymore

They describe a time gone

And a person who has grown.

All the things she did wearing them

Running and falling

Laughing and crying

They should go in the bin I suppose

With other things that are no use

So why are they still here

Like echoes round the mind at bedtime.

If I throw them away

Something may go with them with the rubbish

And somehow they don't deserve that.

Silly really.

122.

It might be the light that brightens

A row of old leaning wooden garages

Down along some dusty backs

Rusty railings splintered by time

Walking to the farm on a sunny morning

Hedges fluttering with little birds

A solitary cow, fly buzzed and munching

The greenest grass near a black pond

Out in the country, dry path leading

Between fields and over the railway

On a fat brick bridge, cold and solid

Weeds high between the tractor tracks

A sky of splendid blueness

Feeding and cleaning out the pigs

In the long iron nissen hut and piggery

Then breakfast in the high kitchen

Bacon, eggs and peppery tomatoes

Out into the bright wide yard

Into a day alive with wonderful prospect

It might have been any of that

But it was something.

123.

Now I'm pushing forty

and the Harley seems quite fast

Maybe time to stop the modelling

I always knew it couldn't last.

The mansion in San Moritz

Is getting to be a bore

And I really can't face going out

With Kate Moss any more

High society parties

No longer float my boat

You can only eat so much caviar

Before it gets stuck in your throat

Jet setting around the world

Mixing with the elite

Sometimes it's hard to keep

The ground beneath my feet

There's only one thing for it

Take off these fancy togs

I'm gooin for a pint int Lion

Proppin' bar up near gents bogs.

124.

Can't cope?, getting worse

Think you're victim of a curse

One eye winking, going lazy

Dog tired, feeling mazy

Restless legs, over thinking

Stress building, over drinking

Can't sleep, wrestling sheets

Counting down your last heartbeats

Hate the neighbours, hate your job

Owing money to the mob

Can't play football, two left feet

Someone sitting in your seat

Girlfriend left and you're still smitten

Get a kitten.

Pacing up and down the room

Seeing visions of your tomb

Lost a tenner found 5p

Locked the door then lost your key

Crashed your car, all your fault

Good times come to a dead halt

Fulfilled life remains unwritten

Get a kitten.

125.

Back street pubs or up some stairs,

A sense of defiance is in the air,

Non conformists, creative geeks,

Fab musicians, clowns and freaks.

Songs you've never heard before,

Curious faces at the door,

Mandolins, guitars, penny whistles,

Banjos, gob irons, fine owd fiddles.

Not attempting to impress,

Just playing art, escaping stress,

In the back rooms, losers, winners,

Pals and strangers, saints and sinners,

You could be in the best hotel in town,

Dressed up dancing to't smoothest sounds,

Mixing with the beautiful elite,

I know where I'd rather be toneet.

126.

Half past six, Wednesday.

It was half past six, it was Wednesday,

Trees were dancing in the breeze

Just me and the dogs sitting on some logs

Resting our weary knees.

When a thought came creeping up on me

Cut me like a stanley knife.

There is no meaning of life.

Well the dogs knew it and the frogs knew it,

That left only me.

Us humans think we're special,

Think we can understand reality.

But as the moments tick tocked past me,

It became so very clear.

It won't really matter when I'm not here.

So we took a stroll through the waving grass

And I threw the dogs a stick.

Dogs ran back in happiness and gave my face a lick.

Ride this moment like a surfboard,

You can never ride it back.

Making plans and promises just before the heart attack.

That was then and this is now,

That moment came and went.

I was there and now I'm here,

And I'm not sure what it meant.

Guide me Mother Nature, alleviate my fear,

Cos it won't really matter when I'm not here.

So I made some tea for the dogs and me,

But we didn't have the same.

That's because the dogs are wild and I've gone really tame.

Ride this moment like a surfboard,

You can never ride it back.

Making plans and promises just before the heart attack.

127.

I waited for the barn owl tonight

But it never came

I had the camera ready and everything

Maybe it doesn't go the same

Way every night

But I think it does

So when it didn't come

I wondered if it was ok

The sky stayed empty as the light faded.

128.

Bat Shit Truth.

If you read the books of history on your shelves,

If you analyse the flags your hopes are tied to.

You'll see the chiefs are working for themselves,

The more you listen, the more you're being lied to.

When the elite say they are trying to save the world,

As they speak at sumptuous banquets and condemn,

The actions of the ordinary people.

While creating laws for you and not for them.

The global mega clubs, the ultra rich,

Design the the techno-future for the masses.

Don't put your faith in them or their ideas,

You mean less to them than broken champagne glasses.

Corporate science, rock icons, film stars,

World Economic Forum, black clad goons.

They fear the billions that they claim to care for,

Stop complying, stop dancing to their tunes.

All the corrupt mainstream media are paid off,

They edit every story with truth pliers.

If an item comes up that detracts from their mantra,

They omit it, they're all dirty little liars.

Tonight when the distant stars are twinkling,

And bats are flitting past and dropping faeces

Look after all your family and your friends

Bats are more honest than most of the human species.

129.

Witchwalking chant. (New song from share of Jan Radovic)

Pressure, troubles piling down

Dreamwalking

Meditate each grassy step

Witchwalking

Ancient paths of glowing gold

Dreamwalking

Megalithic sites of old

Witchwalking

"Solvitar Ambulando"

"It is solved by walking"

40 days and 40 nights

Dreamwalking

Drink the water, holy well

Walk from darkness into dawn

Bare your soul to Nature's might

Step from shadow into light

Leave your worries at the gate

Uncount the time for it is late

Deactivate your raging mind

Secret places you will find

Come with me and chant the tune

Stray beneath the screaming moon

We only have this day you see

Let go of life you will be free.

130.

Ode to a fly.

Right you annoying little bastard

This is your last chance

I've tried being reasonable with you

While you lead me a merry dance

Opened the window said Go bloody go!

Opened front door and back door no bloody show

I know you're doing it on purpose you ugly little git

I know that if I looked like you I wouldn't give a shit

I've rolled up "Take a break" magazine, how could I bloody miss!

You keep landing, crawling, taking off, you're taking the bloody piss

Right, that's it, I'm done being nice, how did you avoid that hit?

You think you're bloody cleverer than me you low life little shit

Now I'm really getting angry, you six legged fat sod

Who gave you all that energy? It didn't come from god

At last! You've flown through't window, end of that buzzing din.

Goodbye, missing you already. Another little bastard flew in!

131.

Displaying one's rear end at the seat of power.

If everything in'tDaily Mail an'tGuardian and the rest

Proves to be pure objective facts.

If everything on'tBBC and ITV and all

Isn't skewed by political contracts.

I'll buy the house next door to Johnny Depp's

And I'll show me arse ont town hall steps.

If Eurovision song contest is always won by t'best

No matter which place they represent.

If politicians never break the rules they make

And none of them dishonourable and bent.

I'll run bollock naked across the Russian Steppes

And I'll show me arse ont town hall steps.

If all our western leaders are honest to the core

And aren't led by t'World Economic Forum

If they really have their people's best interests at heart

And are not controlled by an elite super rich quorum.

My arms are bigger than Arnie's biceps

And I'll show me arse ont town hall steps.

132.

Brave Pal (new song)

You were big and they were slight

You were slow and they were fast

That made them feel superior

But the time of bullies doesn't last.

Brave pal, they made you feel like second best.

Brave pal, you don't follow like the rest.

You are such a faithful friend to me,

You are strong when I am weak.

Your kind heart nurtured in unkindness land.

That is why you are unique.

They all wore the same street uniform

While you wore whatever fit.

All the sniggers and the whispering

Can feel the same as getting hit.

It came as a surprise how strangers act,

You learned life's lessons early on.

Forged in the fire of loneliness,

You would defeat them one by one.

133.

This place is crawling with phantoms. (new song)

This place is crawling with phantoms,

Denizens of a long lost time.

I can sense them in the wall, in the places creatures crawl.

Victims of forgotten crime.

I lie awake in the witching,

Something in the roof above

Are there Sheppeys nesting or a spirit unresting

Moaning unrequited love.

We float suspended in time,

Each moment forms a circle in space

We're neither here nor there

We live in an imaginary place.

This town is teeming with demons

They come out when the working folk sleep.

Autographing cars, vomiting outside of bars.

I pick up papers, I read 'em and weep.

The moon shone coldly last midnight

I ventured out in my cloak

Courting couples kissing, in a speeding car just missing.

Thinking who was that ghostly bloke?

My dogs are telling me something

They look at me with pityful eyes

Maybe i will, maybe I won't

They know something that I don't

I'm waiting for the lord of flies.

A simple light in the morning

Cooly blasts the shadows away.

Somewhere a dead heart beats, think i need to wash my sheets

Preparing for the perfect day.

134.

The first of May - sweet Beltane

The gates of summer unlatching

Light the bonfire, rejoice the buds

Birds from their eggs are a-hatching

Jump o'er the flames, adorn the house

With yellow May flowers and shells

Thornbush and ribbons, gather new wood

Ring out the Beltane bells.

135.

Down and out in Platt Vegas

Runnin out of plans

Sittin int bus shelter

No cash for any cans

Mouth tastes like cat litter tray

Clothes JD sports rags

Trainers worn out, laces snapped

Unpeeling picked up fags

At least its dry and not too cold

And I'm not acting like a fool

Bus goes past, children laugh

I used to go to that school

Funny how things karma out

I passed me 11 plus tha knows

Tommy next to me fast asleep

Snot hangin from his nose.

136.

Get it?

Keats, Van Gogh, Melville, Poe

Burdened by talent, in darkness they strive

Thinking, creating glorious works

Nobody got it when they were alive

Dickinson, Blake, the music of Bach

Passed over by experts, debased by their peers

So far ahead of the humdrum of others

Only mentioned in laughter and jeers

Galileo said earth orbits the sun

For that heresy he was summoned to Rome

Mendel's work on genetics, heredity

Ignored as he sat in his study alone

Do not worry when others ignore you

Or shake their heads, or laugh at your gem

The vast majority of people don't get it

Until somebody else explains it to them.

Doubting themselves those talents continued

Creating for those who have brains of cement

Only when death had quietened their pens

Yes! Finally! Now I know what he meant.

The End.

Copyright Jim Berry 2023.

Printed in Great Britain
by Amazon